NAKIKETAS

AND OTHER POEMS

WALMER POETRY

The Pelican Island by James Montgomery

Poems by Katherine Mansfield

Victory for the Slain by Hugh Lofting

Nakiketas and other poems by May Sinclair

NAKIKETAS

AND OTHER POEMS

by

May Sinclair

SANDNESS
MICHAEL WALMER
2024

Nakiketas and other poems first published 1886 under the pseudonym "Julian Sinclair"

This edition published 2024

by

Michael Walmer
North House
Melby
Sandness
Shetland ZE2 9PL

ISBN 978-0-6457519-4-9 hardcover

"The One remains, the many change and pass;

Heaven's light for ever shines, earth's shadows fly;

Life, like a dome of many-coloured glass,

Stains the white radiance of eternity,

Until death tramples it to fragments, — Die,

If thou wouldst be with that which thou dost seek!"

SHELLEY, *Adonais*

CONTENTS

NAKIKETAS.

LEGEND OF THE KATHA-UPANISHAD.

The Tale of Nakiketas, taught of death.

Vagasravasa Brahman, stern of heart,

But firm in faith, and pious, being learned

In every ancient doctrine; diligent

In the pursuit of works, and punctual

In holiest observances, in prayer

And utterance of sacred syllable;

A worshipper of Vedic word and law —

He, above men in worldly fortune blessed,

In hope to reap reward of righteous deeds,

Vowed sacrifice to the eternal gods

Of all that he possessed; his flocks and herds,

His fair white cattle, peerless steeds, and grain

From all wide-spreading fields of rice and corn —

The double harvest of his golden land

Made fruitful by the wash and overflow

Of mightiest rivers. "All," he vowed, and swore

By the bright face of Agni, the strong arm

Of Indra; then he made a festival

Of sacrifice, and called his guests, and bade

His strong son, Nakiketas, wait on all.

The fair boy, Nakiketas — his one child,

Born of a dear dead love, the only one

Whom his well-ordered heart, that never beat

Save in low rhythm to the appointed hymn,

Dared to hold dear, after the lonely gods;

Beauteous he was, in all the slender strength

Of youth, with its first grace upon his brow,

And hidden in the dark of earnest eyes,

The fire of those young years which sages call

The morning sacrifice of life; his own,

So pure and strong, he loved not to pour forth,

Little by little, in waste offerings —

Had rather kept it as a tranquil pool,

Within whose twilight clearness he might see

Sometimes the faces of the Bright Ones, shades

And faint reflections of invisible things.

His were a soul of wisdom, and a heart

Of tenderness for every living thing;

He cared to wander in the summer shade

Knee-deep in rank grass of the jungle; cared

Beside the lone shores of the monstrous streams

To watch their course, or see the sacred moon

Rise o'er the mighty mountains; every-where

All creatures knew his voice, the timid deer,

And the wild cattle of the woods drew nigh

To his caress; and even beasts of prey,

The hungry tiger and the panther spared

His form, for sake of his unterrified

And fair, familiar looks in passing by.

  And yet at his young heart was care, the gloom

Of one who looks beyond the night and day,

And all the bright appearances of things

For what he knows his eyes shall never see,

Walking as one who grasps in waking hours

After the feeble shadow of a dream.

"Weary am I," he said, "of this slow round

Of days returning, bringing nothing new!

How shall I share my father's drudging life

Of prayer and penance, the tame sacrifice

Of rice, and corn, and fruit, base food and drink,

And cattle's flesh? What boots it? What are we,

To dream the high gods love such offerings?

I know not; but I faint for weariness —

Weary of this unwilling memory,

Bowed with the weight of Vedic words — so sick

Of all the empty sound of Vedic hymns;

Skilled in the verse and measure, in the lore

Of ancient words, I bear the sacred scroll

Of all the Scriptures branded as it were

On my deep soul — no more than others do,

Young scholars sitting at the master's feet.

The wise, the wise who taught us — what are

   they?

Who know no more of death or life than I,

Who know but this — that nothing can be

   known,

Yet dream that there is that which whoso knows,

Passes beyond the dark half of the moon,

Beyond the dwellings of the Bright Ones, they,

The Devas, whom we worship — whom my heart

Tells me shall fail, and fade, and pass away

Before Another, and a Mightier,

As yonder dying moon and lessening stars

Fade in the golden presence of the sun."

   Silent he kept the secrets of his soul,

Told not his kindly teacher, far less told

His father, but with patience ever shared

In service, and strict holding of the rule,

And good works, looking not to the reward.

For days before his father's festival,

Young Nakiketas through the long bright noon

Had watched the reapers reaping, and the beasts

Decked for the sacrifice, as in a dream.

But when he saw the mighty altars raised,

And oil and fuel laid in readiness

To light the fires of that great offering,

And saw the patient victims brought more near,

Ranged in their order — then his soul awoke

Within him, and he cried, "The vow! the vow!

To what unblest Hereafter travelleth he,

Who having sworn with oath to the great gods

To render up his all — his All! keeps back

The dearest offering from the sacrifice?"

   He turned, and in his chamber shut him up;

And thence, arrayed in his costliest

And fairest — purple, scarlet, chains of gold,

Anklets and armlets, gemmed as for a feast,

Went forth, to serve before the bidden guests.

   There, when his father saw him, how he shone

Above his boyhood's grace and loveliness

In gorgeous hues, and jewelled; he waxed wroth,

And cried, rebuking in his anger, "Boy!

Thou meanest insolence to me, and these

My guests; such costly garb and ornament

Beseem a prince — not one who stands to serve.

I deem, Brahmanas! that it is most fit

The young should serve the elder; 'tis my will

This lad, until he be full age, shall stand,

Girt with fair linen round his loins, and wait;

As thou, son, knowest. Thou shalt sacrifice

To-morrow morn at sunrise, for thy sin

Three bushels of white rice, three cakes of corn!"

And Nakiketas heard with patient ears,

And thus, with looks obedient, answered him,

"Thy pardon, lord, as I but thought to pay

The honour due to thy great festival —

Yea, father, yea; a sacrifice I bring."

Silence had fallen on the reverent throng

Of worshippers, and when the piles were laid,

And slaughtered beasts were heaped, and fire was

   lit,

And smoke from those vast altars darkened

   heaven,

Vagasravasa, sacrificing, cried,

"This first to thee, great Brahman! Thee we call!

Let the sweet smoke of this, my sacrifice,

Delight thee, filling thy strong nostrils. Hear!

This unto thee, bright Agni! — this to thee,

Varuna, Vayu, Rudra, and the Twain —

Thee, Pragapati, father! Indra, lord!

'Keep far from us all crooked evil, Thou!

So shall we offer thee the fullest praise!'"

When through the after-silence came a voice,

"Unto what god, oh, father, to what god
Of these thou hailest, wilt thou offer me?"
(And he for very anger answered not.)
"A wretched offering, father, bringest thou,
Of wheat, rice, and fruit; grass-eating kine,
And perishable creatures of the field;
Are these thine 'All?'" **Again, a second time,**
His sire for very anger answered not;
Then Nakiketas waxed more bold, and cried,
"Where is thine oath, oh, father? but this morn
I cried within my heart, 'The vow! the vow!
Surely to worlds unblessed travelleth he
Who, seeking the reward of righteous deeds —
Who having sworn with oath to the great gods,
Makes offerings such as these, and hoards, and
  holds
His dearest treasure from the sacrifice.'
Unto what god, oh, father! to what god
Of all thou hailest, wilt thou offer me?"

The third time, in the ripeness of his wrath,

The pompous sacrificer, outraged, cried,

"Silence, thou dog! I give thee unto death!"

"Great sire, thy will and vow are one; this is

That indestructible — thy promised word."

(He of quick-born and slowly-dying wrath,

Vagasravasa, yet in anger, thus,)

"It is my will! is not the altar there?

— Take him and bind him for the sacrifice!"

    Then strong hands, pitying, yet obedient, laid

Hold on him unresisting, binding him

There, as he stood, where never yet was poured

Blood of so great and goodly offering.

Bound — yet bedecked for sacrifice, he stooped

His forehead to the striker, bowed, and fell.

    Yet Nakiketas — for he prayed this grace,

And it was granted him — a little while

Ere first the blow was struck that slaughtered

    him,

Stood up before them all, and spake these words.

"I have but one message, this — my Teacher —

  go,

Tell him I reverenced him living; now,

Dying, I say to him, 'My happy term

Of years with him is broken and cut off;

Yet let him grieve not, for I think to go

From him unto a greater Teacher' — say,

'That if this be not, yet I gladly sink

To silence after sound of barren words,

From labour to unutterable rest.'"

He came unto the twilight presence-hall

Of hospitable Death, and found therein

No banquet for the uninvited guest,

And Yama, lord of the departed, fled.

For three days and three nights he rested, still

Unsatisfied with food, and on the third,

Lo! Death, returning, found the stranger there;

And, kindly grieved at his unkindly cheer,

Yet spake to prove him, thus, "Say, who art thou

Who, thus unbidden, sittest at my board?

What offering bringest thou from the farther

  shore

Of happy earth?" And Nakiketas wept,

And bowed himself before almighty Death.

"Nought but myself, great Yama! pardon one

Who sought with diligence, but found no thing,

No faith or truth in life that might endure,

Nor perish standing in the sight of Death!"

And Yama, moved, replied, "Nay, stranger, I

Crave rather pardon of an honoured guest

That hath abided cheerless and alone

In house of mine. Therefore I grant three boons

In fair requital — choose, for thou are free."

And Nakiketas pondered, and he saw

No form of any fair desire, but heard

Only the angry words of his vexed sire,

And those stern looks, as he had left them, smote

His spirit's eyesight sore, and thus he prayed,

For his first boon, that they two might be one,

Forgiven each, and loved as formerly.

"Thou cravest a boon already granted thee;

Vagasravasa now, in loneliness,

In ashes, couched on the rough jungle grass,

Mourns his slain son with unavailing prayers."

Then Nakiketas, pondering again —

"This for my second; Yama, I would know

What oft in life has vexed me, what it is,

The great fire-sacrifice which leadeth men

To heaven." And Death told him what it was,

And with what stones men built the altar for it,

And that they signified — these, love and hope;

Those, truth and purity and fortitude.

But for his third he pondered deep and long —

As less uncertain of the thing he wished,

As of the giver's will and power to give.

Then answered boldly, "Lord, for well I know

This place whereon I stand is but the door

Of thy great house; or is an island set

In midst of an unfathomable sea,

Not thy main region and thy continent;

And for I know my soul scarce lives, but lies

As in a dream 'twixt wakening and sleep,

Or betwixt sleep and wakening — tell me, thou,

That which was hidden of old; say, whither wend

The souls of men, and whither the great gods

(For that they pass I know, thou being more

Than they or us), and say how men can gain

The fairest of thine yet unvoyaged lands,

And if my soul shall see it and not die."

The shade of Death grew darker, and he groaned,

"Press me not harder for this fearful boon,

Whose secret hath not slipped my sealèd lips

Since all eternity. Take thou, instead,

A kingdom with the mastery of men,

From Himalaya to the Southern Sea,

Ay, or all Asia from white Caucausus,

With love, delight, and length of lightsome days,

And satisfaction of all sweet desire,

So thou art merciful, to leave this boon."

"Nay — but a gift whereon no dust of earth

Dulleth its splendour, for I know the thoughts

Of earthly things shall die with their desire;

And how shall one receive the gifts of life

From the waste hands of Death?" **(And Death**

    perceived

That the boy, craftier, spied his craftiness.)

"What life taught not, that only would I know!"

"And, if I told, thou couldst not understand;

These things the gods themselves know not. And

    yet

Am I not lord of mine own worlds? Then hear!

Knowledge is Being. Man lives but as he knows.

Men call me Death, who am the messenger

Of one 'fore whom thine own heart told thee true,

The gods should fail and fade and pass away,

E'en as the dying moon and lessening stars

Fade in the golden presence of the Sun;

He is the light within the Sun, the light

Within the eye; the seer and the seen,

Yet he, the same, the Self of all — unseen.

Vainly or well, in his gross element

Man works, and from the clay of his own hands,

Or dreams of his own soul, he shapes the gods.

The gross, the spiritual are cursed alike

In futile faith or coarse idolatry;

Men call me Death — for I am death to these,

Hurling them backward to their mortal wombs,

To die the death they call their life, who love,

Bear children, till their barren fields and toil;

Who pray, and proffer sacrifice and praise,

Who do good deeds with unclean hands, whose
eyes

Lust after the base fruit and recompense

Of righteous dealing, knowing not that Good

Which is itself, as God is god himself,

And hath no lower likeness upon earth.

E'en wise men know him not, whom yet to know

Is life; they change, and pass through many

  births,

Seeking his semblance in the light and shade,

In many forms. He is not found of them

That seek him, but oft godless men, and scorned

Of man, have walked within his light. Ay, found

Not of the prostrate sycophants of heaven,

Not of the singers of the songs of praise,

The sightless worshippers of lords of prayer,

Voice-charmèd hearkeners of Vedic words —

Not of Vagasravasa and his kind."

  This Nakiketas, hearing, wept and groaned.

"Alas, my father! how is thy frail life

In service, in thy penance and thy pain,

Poured, a waste offering on the thankless earth,

Unblest by any god!" "Mourn not for him,

His term shall be renewed. But thou, my son;

Knowledge hath led thy feet through many lands,

And, on the verge of her last continent,

Left thee to madden by the sightless sea.

   Beyond the mighty mountains and the moon,

Beyond the monstrous rivers and the shore,

Beyond the dark and splendour of the sky,

Beyond the dreary border of thy dreams

He dwelleth, Nakiketas, who is known

Only to those who say, 'We know him not.'

Take thou this chain, the token Yama gives

To those who pass to Brahman — and depart;

For thou, my son, hast known him and shalt

   live."

HELEN.

Arthur and Helen: twenty years ago

Their native village knew those names, and all

Knew well their childish forms inseparable.

The gardens where they played lay side by side:

Hers large, but gloomy in the shadows cast

By terrace, wall, and tree; his small, but bright,

A little square where sunshine always fell.

   Each was so welcome in the other's home,

That no day passed wherein their innocent hands

And lips met not in greeting or good-bye;

Until chance parted them — to work unseen,

In either's life, towards a final fate.

First, Helen's father died; and that quick grief

Of widowhood turned grey the mother's hair;

And her new loneliness made strangely grave

The little daughter, and her spirit sank,

While all her love was poured into one stream,

Narrow but deep — a passionless cool fount

Of healing and of comfort to the life

That breathed so painfully beside her own.

Then a swift ruin found them; all their wealth

Was trusted to a stranger, and it sank

In fraudulent adventures of his own.

The mother, helpless in her loneliness,

Felt only that her riches passed from her

(As, under Providence, all earthly things)

Mysteriously, and so struggled not

To weary Justice with the widow's wail,

And fatten richer pockets with her cause;

But faintly drooped, foreseeing sorrows thick

Crowd on the future of the child she loved;

And, powerless against all, she, fearing death

For that dear sake, at last grew sick, and died.

And Helen, still too young to know the least

Of any curse that comes with poverty,

But old enough to feel the utmost grief

That loss by death can give, was left alone,

And trusted to her next of kin, who housed,

Fed, clothed her, and but loved her as they could

   —

And that was little (loveless hearts were they,

Lean, lonely spinsters). She, who could have

  loved,

Had love been asked, shut up her heart, or loved

Nature — her books — her animals — all else

Save men and women; striving all the same

To pay their duty back with hers — no more.

There, in the depths of country quietness,

Where her dull lot was cast, one eye had marked

Her growing beauty: Emile — he it was

(Grown great in speculation, trafficking

In trusts betrayed, and rich with others' loss),

The same who had laid the child's home desolate.

    Led by some chance into her neighbourhood,

He had seen her strange and childish loveliness

Pass by him in the meadows where he fished,

And, turning his slow head — green-hazel eyes,

And thin, dark, lipless face — looked after her.

His narrow gaze drank in her face, her form —

Tall for its thirteen years — her girlish face,

Warm lips and dark eyes set in pallor, hair

That takes the dusk or sunlight of the hour;

All in faint setting of the fading sky,

As, lonely in the level meadow land,

Draped all in black, her form stood dark against

The pale pearl-purple even. Emile had

A sensual eye for beauty, though it were

An angel's, and hers pleased him well. He passed

That night in the still village where she dwelt;

There, learning who her parents were, he planned

A scheme he styled atonement for his crime.

Helen, she knew but of her loss, not how,

Whence, and by whom it came; this ignorance

Would keep his present and his future safe.

His or *her* fortune (it was all the same)

It should be, as it were, but held in trust,

Returned to her at last, and doubled — ay,

Quadrupled; he had laid it out so well!

Where were his blame then? though at first this end

Were unforeseen, yet now the circumstance

Cancelled the crime — she ignorant of aught

Could make the gift less precious in her eyes —

Besides, his private conscience were at peace.

He thirty, she thirteen, or thereabouts;

Four years were ample time, and, if a change

Worked for the worse in that now perfect face,

Why — he had but to leave her: true, the time

And money laid out in the interval

In that case were dead loss; but 'twas, no less,

Like all adventures matrimonial,

A splendid speculation, worth the risk.

He came into her home, he pushed between

Her and her friends, producing shows of right

And claim upon her — speaking of the dead

Whom he had wronged, "He knew, he loved them
  well,

As he had cause to; did they never know

That Helen's father, ere his death, had made

Himself the guardian of his child? He grieved

That other cares had held him back so long

From some fulfilment of a debt he owed

To that dead man." He flattered, he cajoled

Their simple hearts, they knowing never more
Than Helen who he was who flattered them;
And so he gained his point, and left them glad,
And garrulously murmuring gratitude.
  Then Helen went to school, and all that gold
Could buy of knowledge became hers — and
    more;
For she grew into girlhood, nourishing
A mind and spirit, born most beautiful,
With beauty of the fields, and woods, and lanes,
Of all things round her own still life, as well
As with pure thoughts and glorious images
Of dreams that made a life within her own.
  From time to time he saw her, and he strove
To gain her love with presents — ornaments
Golden and jewelled — costly clothes, which she
Should wear to make her lovely in his sight:
For, though the lust of gold so ruled his life,
He had passions which o'erruled that one; he

loved

To spend, not hoard, his treasure, and could be

Princely in lowest pleasures.

                                               But he saw

No love come for his gifts; she thanked him,

   praised

His jewels, put them on to please his eye,

But it seemed not they pleased her own. At last

His cunning grew aware of this, and then

He brought her books instead, and spoke of them

Nobly, for he could summon noble words

Lightly to his false lips, and clothe in them

Grand thoughts, remembered — born not of his

   brain.

He praised the poets whom she loved; he read

Aloud to her, and let them speak for him;

For he had art to make his voice vibrate

With tenderness and meaning not his own.

Then they would sit together; if she turned

The talk from trivial things, he also veered,

And spoke of life — death — God — the mystery

That rounds man's knowledge; opening to her

  eyes,

Through his thin thought, dim visions infinite,

Beyond it far: "They two would sublimate

Their mutual creeds above all other; he

Would be th' apostle of a fairer faith

To her;" and so she listened, and he sowed

A scanty seed of knowledge in her mind,

That, taking root in that more generous soul,

Grew up, a larger and a fairer flower.

  For he had science, and a certain sense,

Acquired and cultured, of things beautiful;

And lightly on the surface of belief

His trivial mind skimmed, touching here and

  there,

Approving and rejecting, shaking off

A passing gleam of light from its thin wings;

But, where the heart of man had ever loved —

Believed — hoped — striven in earnest ecstasy

The keen small sight failed; cynic nescience

Embittered the mean mind that made itself

The measure of all things — too apt to test

All, in his own false heart he had weighed the

  world,

And found it wanting. Had it not been so,

He might have seen how long since how all her

  heart,

Her childish heart, her faith, and reverence

Were given to him; but his eyes were blind

Unto the secret signs of such a love —

Love, made so lowly by its gratitude,

That it lived on without a hope, or thought

Of far fulfilment — love all satisfied

To be his friend, sit by him, hear him speak —

Too simple to suspect or hope for more.

  And, all the time he ordered that the child

Should pass her days close hidden in her school,

Or in the quiet of her village home,

Where she could make no further friends, and

  nought

Be dearer than the pleasure and surprise

His coming gave her — so that he might be

Her all in all, the one thought of her life.

So, hastening to fulfilment of his plans,

In the fourth summer since they first had met,

He came, resolved to win her for his wife.

Not once in all that time he had asked his heart

Whether he loved her, or had guessed her love;

Took it for granted — or but cared to see

The promise of her beauty ripening more

Into the perfect type of womanhood,

And feel that here again his choice of chance

Had proved successful, as it ever had.

  This time his talk was of himself: he made

A short sketch of his life — he spoke of death,

Of friends long dead, or dead to him (no fault

Of his, God knew!) — spoke of his wasted life —

His wish for better things; then, looking up,

He saw her tearful eyes, and, half-amused,

Learnt the full secret of a love that lay

So far outside the reckoning of his plans;

'Twas just as well, and made it easier

To take her hand, and ask her, "Could she love

A broken heart, made bitter by the world? —

'Twas all he had to give." Poor child, she wept

A little while; then, trembling, told him all

Her love and faith, and of her former fear

Lest there should be presumption in her love

That made her hide it from his sight alway.

  And then the ring he had bought in view of this,

The heavy jewelled ring, was shown, and slipped

On her slight finger, and she swore to be

"Faithfully his, for ever — evermore!"

Meanwhile her child-friend, in his distant home,

Had grown to manhood — older by four years

Than she — and while to her his face became

Only a far-off memory, and no more,

He had been ever used to picture hers

Grown to full beauty, bearing still the traits

Of its sweet childhood; for her portrait hung

Still in his father's house beside his own,

And kept her image bright, reminding him

Of her, as of a sister. Ten long years

Had passed since each had seen the other's face;

Then Arthur heard of Helen, by some chance

Meeting with one who knew her in her home,

And (pleased with one so brightly versatile —

Bounteous to give and eager to receive

Of all things beautiful — a chance surprise

Of lustrous colour and swift-moving grace,

Among stiff types of dull society —

Cold-marbled casts and statuettes of man)

The stranger asked him down to stay with him,

For boating in that lonely neighbourhood.

And so it came that Helen, as she sat,

One evening, in the dingy parlour's dusk,

Was startled by a shadow, that across

The well-known forms within her window-pane

Fell, blotting them for a moment — flower and
    tree,

Dark hedge, and little square of twilight sky;

And then a name was spoken at the door,

A half-remembered name, that brought to her

Things long-forgotten, fancies that belonged

To her young life, now left so far behind.

Then Arthur entered, and he took the hands

Now strangely firm and white, that used to press

Warm in his own, browned with their summer
    play,

And spoke her old name gently, wondering,

With reverence, at her maiden loveliness.

  Whether her year's betrothal seemed too long,
Or shade of disappointment in her love,
Or him she loved, had fallen on her life,
But Arthur saw, or fancied that he saw
Some sorrow glooming through the bright
  disguise
Of all her courtesy of smile and laugh,
And questioning of him and of his home,
But guessed no cause. And then the maiden aunts
Came in, and sat between him and the light
Of Helen's face that brightened their dark room;
They spoke no word of her, or of her love —
That was a secret they were charged to keep —
But chattered till their voices silenced her,
And Arthur, wearying of them, took his leave.

But the next day, and still the next, he came,
And lingered in the place the summer through,

Making new friendships everywhere, and pressed

On every side to stay, until his form,

His face, his voice were known in every house

In all the country round; and none could guess

What made him love the dreary place so well.

And Helen came to feel a certain sense

Of pleasure in his presence, day by day;

And Arthur, seeing that her looks were bright,

And gladder at his coming, struggled not

Against his love, but let it conquer him,

And bear him captive to an unknown fate.

And Helen, with no consciousness of doom,

Gave to his love, in very innocence,

The hope it longed for: "Had not Arthur been

Her friend, dear as a brother, long before?

Was he not son of her dead father's friend —

Loved only for the sake of homelier love?"

But when the summer passed, and he had gone,

She asked her heart in silence, had she felt

Too much joy at his coming, too much pain

At parting? — maybe overmuch — but all

Was over now; and he would come no more.

  The sullen winter came, and found her sad,

And brought her own betrothed, and passed

  away;

And she had prayed Emile that they might wed,

Not yet, but in the sunniest summer-time.

But with the spring came Arthur back again,

Came, seeking her dear presence more and more;

Came, with the voice that touched, the look that

  searched

Her spirit; with some master influence Charming

it more and more within his sphere.

And Emile also came, and found a fault

Grown since he left her — too much unreserve —

Enthusiasm — unseemly earnestness

He hated in a lady, and his wife.

And she too, grieving, felt some secret change

In him she loved, some lapse of tenderness,

Of insight, sympathy; he seemed more dull;

There was some falling-off in that fine part

He played before — she knew not where it lay;

But to herself she owned that Arthur *was*

All that Emile had only *seemed* to be, —

Seeing some likeness in their cast of thought,

Through all unlikeness in their characters.

She vexed her heart with questions:— "Did it beat

More passionately, hearing Arthur come,

Than at Emile's slow step — his voice — his kiss?

Were not her admiration and belief

A little more for Arthur than Emile?

What was the meaning of that growing power,

That sway of his opinion over hers?

Was then her heart too little for them both,

That friendship should be falsehood unto love?"

How could she fail to feel that difference?

Emile — his mind a cold, self-centred gloom;

His eyes, half-blind with gazing on the dark

His own long shadow made upon his path;

And Arthur — one whose eager youth had dared

To claim from life the utmost life can give;

Knowledge was his — his spirit upon all

Pouring its swift and intense light, drew forth

Innumerable colours, and rejoiced

In all the changing splendour that it made;

Too passionate in pursuit of truth to be

Of one opinion long — unknown to him

Life's awful cause and meaning, he became

As one who only feels the passion, hears

The music — accent — eloquent rhythm, and

   pause

Of some old language that he knows not; power

Was his, and pleasure, and th' approving love

And praises of the world; and yet withal

He had grown pure and strong, and crowned his
   youth

With victory thus early — holding back

A passionate heart from ruinous desires.

And yet she knew no diff'rence in her love

And gratitude; no pause, no lapse, no wrong;

But — whether 'twas that she had asked too
   much

Of Emile's "broken heart," or sought and touched

The cold hard ground beneath that shallow
   stream

Of sophistry, and that her passionate heart

Was wounded in repulsion and recoil —

Her sweet, dependent reverence and belief,

That made her love to change her thought for his,

Had ceased to be. Oh! she was ignorant —

She knew not that her love and faith were one,

Born with one birth-throe, dying in one death;

She knew not that the struggling will can give

A strange, unreal life within the mind

To passion that has died from out the heart;

While that a new quick soul of love can beat

Hidden beside the dying or the dead;

She knew not — till she found, from day to day,

The working in her mind of some excuse

Made to itself for lack of tenderness

Towards her lover. "He had grown so cold

Of late; it was not right that she should woo,

Where Emile was indiff'rent." Then remorse

Would come — she forced her feelings, and her
  love

Lived on awhile as pity, gratitude

That thrilled far more at memories of the past,

Than at touches of his presence; moved

At sight of gifts sent long ago; at thought

Of all his kindness — of his wasted life —

And of his need of her.

                                And then, too late,

She felt the birth-pang of that larger love

Strike to her soul with agony and shame;

And in her pain she cried: "Oh! I have sinned

Against all love and faith and honour — false,

Falser than any heart that ever broke

Its love's light oath in girlish wantonness,

E'en as I held myself so far above

My weaker sisters' fault of fickleness!"

Yet — 'twas but passion — still her will might
  rise

And stamp it out, reclaiming the lost love;

He need not know her faithlessness, her life

Should with long sacrifice redeem the wrong

Done in a moment's madness.

                                This one thought

Possessed her, of redemption for her fault;

And from that hour she swore to turn her back

On Arthur — so to shut him from her life,

That nevermore his voice, his smile should break

Its penitential gloom. So, when he came,

She made excuse, and would not see him then;

And, if he saw her, or by chance they met,

She tried to shun him, scarce would speak to him.

And then a letter from his mother came,

Praying her, "for the love of other days —

For love of her dear son — to come to her;"

And, weeping bitterly, she wrote again,

Thanking so dearly; but refusing her.

  And Arthur saw, and wondered at the change;

Then had a dream of her that troubled him;

He dreamt that she was drowning; that he saw

Dim fields all riven with swift-rushing streams;

While white and fair her body lay upon

The dusky tide — bearing her far from him;

And while with faint and stumbling knees he

  pressed

Unto her rescue, other hands than his

Snatched her from that swift death; but, on the

  banks,

Shackled with rusty chains her tender wrists,

And led her through the darkness of the fields

Far — a faint image in his fading dream;

And still the horror grew, until the stir

And delicate light scent of morning stole

Into his slumber, wakening, and he rose;

And that day, trembling with the strength and

  fear

Of his resolve, went forth, and praying her

To see him but this once, he told his love.

And she, who never once had dreamed of this,

Stunned, as by news of death, at first was dumb,

And listened, trembling, holding back her breath;

Then shrinking from him, answered, stammering

  low:

"Leave me — it is too late! it — is too late!"

"Why, Helen?" "Why — because my love is
   sworn

Already — oh, how doubly false I am —

To him — to you! and yet — I knew it not.

I tried — oh, Arthur! turn not from me — speak!"

He answered, "If I knew you not so well,

Reproaches could be ready in my mouth

For pain you might have spared — but let that
   pass —

I will not plague you with a vain complaint;

How could you tell me that you were not free

To be so loved? — 'tis I who am to blame

For ling'ring near you — ah! too late and long."

Then Helen (feeling only in her shame

It were less hard to hear him swear, and scold,

And call her the worst jilt that ever fooled

With a life's passion for her pastime — ay,

That his worst anger could be better braved

Than this dread sorrow of his tenderness).

Praying for his forgiveness, told him all —

How she had let her love for him destroy

Her faith in Emile — striving, as she told,

To give herself more blame, the more she screened

And covered his unworthiness with praise.

And Arthur heard in silence to the end;

But when she told him of her wedding-day —

A month hence — uttering then her lover's name,

He rose with sudden passion, and cried out,

"God! I could bear it if it were not he!

Helen, it must not be — I know this man —

I care not to revile him; but, believe,

I were content to go my separate way,

Sworn never more to see your face again,

So that I knew you not this rascal's wife!

I plead not for myself, but I would save,

E'en if I loved you not, your life from wrong."

She listened, trembling; while the bitterness

Of Arthur's words sank deep into her heart,

There mingling with her own more vague
    mistrust

Of Emile; and she answered timidly,

"What wrong? you say you know him — how is
    that?

What can you mean by this mysterious blame?"

"Dearest, alas! what shall I tell you then?

I come from London, from the very world

Wherein he has made himself a name, that's
    known

Too well by all, and in the cleaner mouths

Of all his fellow-merchants named with scorn

And execration; of the rest, my lips

Could hint not to a woman, least to you."

"Arthur, it may be (if you know the truth) —

It may be he has erred, but love is strong

To save, to win from evil the dear heart

Which is its own; this much I owe to him;

Though I have fallen far from love's pure type,

If I do this, e'en yet I may be true."

"Helen, you *have* been true, beyond all bounds

Of human truthfulness: did *he* not take

A mean advantage, in his selfishness,

Binding the childish heart that knew not love?

Not as a sophist, arguing for himself,

But as a brother, pleading for your life,

I do implore you, tell him all the truth

(You say yourself your love for him is past),

And leave him to his own unworthiness."

"Oh, Arthur! hold me not from that last good!

It must be done — it must. I loved him, too,

Once, long ago — he thinks I love him still!"

She paused; her tears came slowly, painfully;

Which Arthur seeing, took her hand in his,

And gently answered, "Listen, dearest, see —

There is no marriage where there is no love —

No love, believe me, without joy, and hope,

And faith, and perfect trust of each in each;

And faith there cannot be, except for good

Longed for, and found in the beloved. Oh! true

And tender little heart! I see it all —

Since these things were not, and have never been,

You nobly think to crystallise your love

Into a cold clear virtue, beautiful —

A jewel for his wearing! Only prove

The dangerous issue — live to see him tread,

Hog-like, your duty to the dust! Oh, God!

What base conclusion! *you* to waste and spill

The pure wine of your life, poured out to crown

The earthy cups that satiate that brute,

That clod! — disgusting!" **As he stopped, she snatched,**

Stammering with anger, her hot hand from his,

And answered passionately, "'Tis shameful — this!

I am not sunk so low that I will stand

And listen to such words, and yet be calm;

Surely the heart that loved him must know more

Of what he is than any stranger can —

I loved him! Yet I blame you not, you speak

Only the scandals you have heard — no more;

You know not of his goodness — else untrue

And cowardly your words were. Gratitude —

Is it nothing? Shall his kindness lay no claim

To my false heart? — yet true, to scorn the lies

That falser slander breathes against him! Go!"

(He started, and a quiver of quick pain

Went through him, but he moved not from her

  side,

Nor grew his eyes less tender, looking down

Calmly upon her passion, till the end.)

She paused; then in her loneliness she drew

Nearer: "Oh God! the tears are in your eyes.

My love — my love, lost evermore to me!

Oh! speak not so that I must answer you

In anger, or my heart will break. Forgive,

Forgive me once, then leave me. I am strong

Now, but a later hour may find me weak.

Think not I shall be wretched, for I know

That love is *not* the whole of woman's life,

Nor yet of man's, but there are higher things —

Devotion — honour — faith — self-sacrifice.

Think, dearest, though I may not be your wife,

Our love shall still be with us, and shall move

To far-off purer ends, and unforeseen.

Forget me, Arthur — you may love again,

And be more blessed than I am; finding out

A path where love and duty are at one.

And now, 'tis best that we should say good-bye."

But Arthur, turning from her, answered low:

"Would I were dead, for such sharp agony

With some has died in death, as easily

My heart could break, but that I choose to live,

Not for the dread of death, but for your sake,

And for a distant hope that will not die.

Yet — since you will not be my wife — but say

I may be near you in your utmost need;

And when your voice shall call me, I will come;

Promise me, Helen," — and she promised him.

　He would have lingered out that bitter hour

In dread of parting, but for some slight stir

Without — a step, a voice, a slender sense

That pricked the fainting will.

　　　　　　　　　　He looked at her

In reverence a moment, as he had looked

Last year, when first he saw her. Then their lips

Kissed in a passionate silence, with no word

Of parting said, his presence and his form

Passed from her — the one splendour of her life

Parted in dream-like twilight, as it came.

And she — she only shuddered as she felt

His passing in the garden throw a gloom

Of sudden shadow 'cross the window-pane.

But in her own dark chamber's loneliness

She struggled with her passion; on her bed

Tossing in torment — in her very dreams

Two voices called, two faces looked at her;

And all the mad desire of love cried out,

In pain, against compassion and remorse;

Each night more wild, and still more terrible

That night before her marriage morning dawned.

But with its sun she rose more calm and strong,

And strangely passionless, and so was wed.

   She saw no dark injustice in her life,

Through all Emile's indiff'rence, up to this

Her doom of loveless marriage, when her eyes

Were turned from his who loved her evermore —

Saw but the fiery arms of sacrifice

Stretched out to draw her to the altar; saw

Her victory, her flame-crowned martyrdom.

She passed, with that dark presence at her side,

Far from the pleasant land where she was born;

Where she had loved and suffered; where her love

Dwelt somewhere in some spot unknown to her.

Then, from a year of travel, came again

To some dark city mansion for her home;

And the still village knew her face no more.

There — through long months of misery — her
    doom

Closed in, and gathered to its deadly end.

He (who had looked upon her as he might

On some rich picture which his wealth had
    bought

To sate his sense with its dark loveliness)

First grew aware of something in the depths

Of her still nature greater than his own;

(Thought, this was talent, it would make her
    shine

The brighter in those circles where he meant

Her star should move beside his lesser light,

Shedding a glory on his mind who made

Choice of this splendid spirit for its mate;

But, though he called her "cleverer" than himself,

Her cared not that the world should think her so;

There, lest her radiance should eclipse his own,

She should shine bright or dimly at his will);

Then grew to fear her for the thing he praised.

Her intellect, her truth, her purity

Were as an outer conscience, troubling him

More than his own — seeming to prove him dull,

Shallow, near-sighted — while again, her eyes

Shamed him; most surely, if she once knew all,

Such eyes could strike and scathe him with their

   scorn!

Then fear begot slow hate, and hate revenge,

Tempered by fear, and daring but to work

In mean affront — slights, taunts, indignities

Too small for pride's resentment.

                         Then came worse —

Their country gossip, brought by Arthur's friends

And hers, became a London scandal — spread,

Linking her name with Arthur's, whispering

Of secret dearness in their past — and more:

"He was her lover once, that much was known–"

"It was disgraceful — for 'twas she began

The thing — she was the wooer, not the woo'd–"

"There was no harm in the young man himself —

Tall, handsome, therefore she could find no fault

But that of poverty; so she was false,

And cast him from her for a richer chance —"

"Married for money, she deserved her fate —"

"One more faith-breaking, beauteous, heartless

    jilt!"

But Helen winced not at their voices, swerved,

Or mourned the madness of her martyrdom;

She only grew more still, more cold, more calm,

Knew less and less of passion and regret

Till the end came.

        The swift doom tarried not;

But in the third year of their marriage fell —

Closing its agony with shame and death.

Emile was ruined! Some more monstrous snare,

Set for another's ruin, had sprung back

Upon the fowler, and o'erthrown him. News

Came of his failure and his infamy.

It was at midnight that it came, and they

Late come from some gay dance or theatre,

There in the sunken lamplight of the room

They entered first, the message met their sight.

He read — he sat with fearful eyes that veered

To every side, with hot uncertain hands

That plucked and fingered trifles in their way —

Then mad with all despair, he rose and cursed,

And stamping, shook the velvet-covered floor

Of that dim chamber. And she read it too —

Looked on his rage with gentle dignity;

Then, with one thought of supreme sacrifice,

Moved forward, put her hand upon his breast,

And said, "I will go with you — let my love

Be near you now;" but he — the wounded brute

—

Shrunk for a moment from the eyes he feared,

Then in his madness raised his arm and struck —

Struck at her jewelled breast a deadly blow;

Then, turning in his horror, fled from her —

Fled from her death, and from his own disgrace.

And she — she knew not, fainting in her pain,

What else befell, until she found herself

In servant hands that nursed, and heard awhile

Voices around her bed, and felt the touch

Of half-warm lips against her wounded breast,

And heard the pitying murmur, "It is dead."

And then her heart knew all — remembering

all;

And as she pined and fretted, fever came,

And horror visited her brain — for then

Ever the swaying shadow of a man

Hung on her chamber-wall before her eyes;

For so (if death set free some fearful dream,

Born of the dying, to be his messenger

Unto the living brain) the tale was told

Of that vexed spirit that had sought to fly

Down to the dark of death from life's disgrace.

Later, the fever ceased, but they who nursed

Knew that it passed to leave but room for death,

And told her so, and asked her, "Was there aught

Would comfort her?" And, Helen, turning slow

Her feeble eyes upon the awful past,

Bethought her dimly of a voice, that said,

"Call to me in your need, and I will come;"

And told her longing, and they, wondering,

But loth to cross her wish in that last hour,

Sought out, and sent for Arthur; and he came,

Travelling through midnight to his love.

Too late

For all save speechless parting; for her look

In passing; for the touch of helpless hands,

And awful kiss from cooling lips of death;

Then parted, with no token of his love,

Till they who nursed her, grieving, gave one tress

In smoothing her black hair for burial.

Slander and ignorance have linked her name

With falsehood and worse wrong; the world's sick

  eye

Visioned dark blots upon the purity

Of her white wedding garment and her shroud,

And o'er her memory has fallen gloom

Out-blackening death's shadow.

Only one

Lives who knows all — who knows that Love,

e'en lost,

Still rules this Fate of ours to noblest ends —

He, unto whom, through death, she is become

The bridal spirit of his life — unseen,

But powerful in blessing — he who gained

These for his love — one curl of her dark hair,

The pressure of her dying lips — no more.

APOLLODORUS.

Not in our days, and in another land

Than ours, a land where softlier fell the feet

Of fairer seasons, and the harmless years

Left the bright wilderness unspoiled, to be

The bourne and birthplace of all loveliness;

A land of light, and yet mysterious

With the pine forest's purple mist and maze;

A pleasant summer land, still pastoral

In streams of unstained water, musical

With reeded margins where the sweet wind sang,

In green and golden fields, whose light was given

Not from the scant rays of a churlish star,

Distant and cloud-enfolded, but indeed

From a most beautiful and bounteous sun,

That bared his skies to fill them but the more

With beauty and gladness, or that took his veil

Of vapour, but to flush the land and sea

With hues more gorgeous than his own pure

  beams;

A quiet land, but not unpopulous,

With gentle flocks and gentler shepherd men.

Here dwelt the sweetest singer of his time,

The young Apollodorus, unto whom

Love gave his first fair fellowship; with him

All thought and passion, life and love were one,

And one their object — 'twas a maid, whose face

E'en in his infant dreams, bent dimly o'er

His cradle, dimly beautiful; who grew

With his young life more fair, and led him on,

With looks as childlike as his own, to love,

And ever seek her bright companionship;

And wondrous stories of old time she knew,

And told him, tutoring in mystic lore,

In greybeard fable, wisdom infantine,

Of years wherein the wizard world was young;

Till rough hands rent him from her, and a scroll

Was given him, and he was bound and bent

Over its characters, and heard no more

The maiden's legends; and her face was shut

Out of his days. But, though her saw her not,

He felt her presence with him in the night,

And heard her voice call to him, as it were,

For ever eastward through a twilight land.

Yet it befell that in a pleasant time

The bands that bound Apollodorus broke,

And that dull scroll was taken from his sight;

And he, a singer with his songs unsung,

Unset to any music, lute, or lyre,

Or simple river-reed, went wandering

All in the summer land at dawning, sad

And weary, seeking for he knew not what,

Aye following an eastward-flowing stream;

When from the twilight hills, his splendour split

In the full stream, bright, cloudless, and alone,

A fearful light that deadened his own dawn,

Out of the east arose the mighty sun;

And eastward, eastward rang the voice he knew.

Thither he followed, followed, finding naught;

But his own shadow mocked him on the grass,

And his own likeness mocked him in the stream;

Eastward he followed, as the river ran,

Pursuing the faint sweetness of the sound

That near along the reed-tops, and more far,

From o'er the meadows, o'er the twilight hills,

Lured him, until the rushing river ran

Hot underneath the faint hot sky at noon;

Lured him, until the silent-circling stream

And he looked westward at the setting sun.

Then in a desperate utterance he spoke —

"Die, my faint songs, for I shall never know
That mortal music which whoever hears
Weds his sweet words with sweeter melody;
Die, my faint songs! as I shall die, for love
Of yon far voice that dies upon the stream."
He ceased, and in the silence of the shore
He heard the reed-tops' breathless preluding,
And then a song that made the hearkening air
Throb with its passionate pulses, sweet but sad,
Sadder than murmurs of a voiceless lyre
Touched by the hands of one whose lips are
    dumb,
And know no language. In his wonderment
Apollodorus paused; and following not,
As fearful of the former mockery,
Lo! his own shadow faded on the grass,
And his own likeness fainted on the stream,
And he beheld the form of her he loved;
And as her singing ceased not, to his lips

Rose all his mighty song, to wed itself

With her most wild and wordless melody,

Complete in happy cadence; and he knew

That songs of his should live for evermore,

Sweet-married to the music of love.

The same, and yet not all the same was she,

But changed, and with a fearful semblance

   grown

More great, more wonderfully feminine;

For, as low sun-fire stains the air, he saw

From vermeil veins a light incarnadine

Flush her full limbs and fire her lips more fair

With living splendour; while her bright locks

   shone

Like wild rays heavenward reared; and her blue

   eyes

Were dimmed with violet-dusk like that which

   swims

In shadows on the summer seas. It seemed

The dimness of her ancient mystery

Was passed, for on her brow there shone the

  light

Of gladness, and her countenance expressed

The sweetness of a more familiar grace.

And thus, still singing, with her hands she

  signed,

And young Apollodorus followed far,

Where'er her steps might lead; with that sweet

  song,

Their prothalamium.

For, evermore

He knew her presence in the pastoral fields,

Or by the circling of the silent stream,

Or in the forests' purple mist and maze;

And love was with him in the summer land,

Where, in the light of happy hours that passed

Flower-crowned and flushed with glory, bearing

each

The proper splendour of her season's prime,

He dwelt, the sweetest singer in the land;

And there he sang that song of his he called

"The Song of Life."

And yet he sang of her;

The secret song of all sweet things that be

Betwixt the bitterness of birth and death;

Sang how it was her voice alone he heard

At even in the whispers of the stream,

Or in the sea-voice of the moaning pines,

At morning in the happy murmuring

Of living things; he sang that everywhere,

In all fair forms that move on earth, he saw

The likeness of her beauty; that the light

Of her clear eyes was sight within his own,

And that her love was life within his limbs,

And hers the sacred secret of his song,

Learnt from the mystic music of her lips,

Whereto his own lent language; and so set —

Soul to the soulless — wedded minstrelsy

Bore beauty from the barrenness of sound.

Thus for a triad of bright years that clad

His youth with strength and beauty, triumphed

  he;

Until an hour, that came in the sad train

Of that last month that with her golden head

Bowed down goes forth to meet the winter wan,

Reached him the crown of manhood, intertwined

With laurel wreath of lyric victory;

And in his heart the hope and longing grew

To leave that maiden in the summer land,

And pass beyond the twilight hills, and there

Sojourn a season, striving with his song

To win himself a mightier acclaim,

And with the praises of his love to make

Her loveliness the more beloved of men;

But when he told her of his great desire,

Saying, "Dear love, I leave thee; fare thee well;

I go beyond the twilight hills, beyond

The river sources of this land, to seek

Another country, while I leave thee here;

But for a while I go; and thou wilt wait

Here my home-coming — 'tis but for a while."

She answered, "No; thou canst not leave me, love;

Not leave, so long as thou dost love — think'st thou

I should await thee? Nay; but rather go

Where'er thou goest, following thy feet;

For I will be thy shadow on the hills,

Thy image in the sources of the stream

For aye, as long as thou and I are one;

As long as thou dost love thou canst not say

'Farewell;'" and, as he still importunate prayed,

Still more importunate she answered him,

Until she conquered him, and left for dead

That hope within his heart.

                The self-same night

He dreamt of her; he dreamt he passed beyond

The hills, and saw the birthplace of the streams

Of his own land, and by their sources sat

The maiden of his love, before a wheel,

Winding a fearful woof of her own hair,

And singing as she span; while evermore

The whirring and the noise of that great wheel

Made dim her delicate music; in the woof

Was wrought a running pattern, stars and suns,

And crescents, shapes of birds and beasts and

   flowers,

With their own hues — work of such

   wonderment

That all amazed he woke, to see the dawn

Pale o'er the twilight hills, and told the maid

What had befallen; and she counselled him,

"Fear not to dream of me, but sleep to-night;
And if thy dream should come again, look well;
For wrought and charactered within the woof
There is a riddle thou mayst read." That night
He slept, and dreamt again the self-same dream,
And so bethought him of her counselling,
That he looked well to the device, and read
These words, encharactered through warp and
  woof,
"Thou knowest me not. I am not that I seem;"
And waking with the dawn, he asked the maid
Whether he had interpreted aright
The meaning of the ciphers and the signs.
"Right and not right," she answered; "hast thou
  read;
Read thou no more; thrice comes the dream
  maybe,
But love, and fear not, thou, for I am thine."
And the third time he dreamt the self-same

   dream,

This night with added horror — for, behold!

The mighty woof flowed downward from her

   form,

And carpeted the ground, and rose again

On every side close-woven like a wall

Of pictured tapestry; while louder grew

The whirring of her monstrous wheel, more vast

The fearful web, that seemed to clutch and wrap

Live creatures in its folds like summer flies;

And as she swifter span, there as he stood

Wove o'er and wrapped him shroudlike, horrible;

Till blinded, pinioned, strangling, he awoke.

That day he spoke not of his dream, for dread

And very horror; and he shunned that maid,

Fearing her face, that seemed to wax and wane

For ever like her likeness of the dream —

Fateful and death-like. He would wander wild

In solitary places, loathing love,

And her alike.

                  And there his brain grew sick,

And, all dream-haunted, warped the weakling

  sight

To its own phantasy. She came to him

At times, in all her ancient loveliness

He saw her, hand-in-hand with Sin, go down

To dance with Death before the gates of hell,

Or stand, a thing diseased, whose leprous breasts

Nourished a hideous brood — deformities

And shapes of sin-begotten sickliness;

And all the fair appearances of earth

And sky were changed; the fogs of autumn hung

Thick-stagnant o'er the lowering land; it seemed

To west and east a blood-red river ran

Of sunset and a cruel dawn, made dim

With purple vapours of the sickly breath

And poison-damp of cities; and he pined,

For all the fruit of autumn's garnering

Was bitter to his tongue, and ripening ears

Of wheat or barley black with rottenness;

And as he pined, he pondered o'er and o'er

The meaning of his dreams, and that he read

Symbolic, interwoven, with the words

"Thou knowest me not. I am not that I seem."

Thus, after having brooded many days,

The busy brain made meaning horrible

Out of the wreck of its own phantasy,

And he came back to her, and standing wide

Aloof, gave utterance, in his agony:

"Flee from me, fair one! wherefore tarryest thou

To toy with Death? is he not tenderer,

Fairer than I? Think'st thou I care to hold

My heart from loathing of thy loveliness

To taste thy kisses' poison? Woe is me!

With treacherous secresy didst thou beguile

My heart with subtle seeming. What is this —

'Thou knowest me not. I am not that I seem?'

Nay — that thou art not, yet I know thee well,

As false, and falser in thy seeming fair

Art thou! and I — what would I have but
  Truth?

Better a bald and shameless truth than thou —

A falsehood clothed with semblance! Fare thee
  well,

I will not love thee more!" E'en as he spoke —

With ruthless words renouncing the sweet hope

Of coming days, and cancelling the joy

Of days long gone — she turned and fled from
  him,

Leaving his heart as vacant as the soul

Leaves the dead body, and the self-same night

He felt her presence failing from the fields,

Nor evermore heard echoes of her voice

At even in the whispers of the stream,

Nor in the sea-voice of the moaning pines.

And now, Love being gone, life too had fled
To follow him, and very death had come
To claim the poet as his own, had sleep
Not sent a ministering dream to ply
The functions of true life within the soul,
And keep the heart-blood flowing; for he lay
Long hours in a deep trance, and seeming dead
To all sweet light and sound, and his weak hand
Lay nerveless on his lyre. Before the dawn,
Betwixt long sleep and wakening, he grew 'ware
Of an imperfect presence, shadowing
The depths of dream; and half in weariness
He turned towards a gentle light that stole
Under his sunken eyelids, lifting them;
And eastward-looking he awoke. And lo!
The dense earth that he lay on, and the light
Of dawning failing from his consciousness,
Sense was not, and the spirit's sight was filled
With the perfection of a single form —

Dark, with a melancholy mystery,

Was that phantasmal presence, but within

Of such sufficing splendour, that it seemed

She stood in the dim light of her own eyes,

And needed not the sunset or the dawn

To lighten her; clothed was she, not alone

With her black hair, but veiled from head to

  foot,

And all her fearful beauty darkened through

A dim and purple-paling woof, like those

Wind-woven from the sunless clouds; the robe

Was wrought upon the border and the hem

With many a sacred character and sign,

And symbol arabesque, in gold device,

Which whoso learns to read shall learn the lore

Of Indian and Egyptian sages. Fear,

And love consuming fear, by turns pursued

Their swift course through Apollodorus' soul;

And as he moved his passionate arms to grasp

The border of her veil, he feared her gone,

Feeling the formless air, till once again

She came, then faded; and the solid earth

And the dull light of dawning were restored;

And in the former landscape of his life

He stood, while nought of former things

   remained

Save a wan memory.

                Then he arose,

And took his lyre; and, wandering, he sang

Of divine things, of beauty and love, unborn

From earthly touches; of the light supreme

That needeth not to struggle from the sun

Through eyesight to the soul, but is in man

A light of all light, after which there shine

All splendours of the earth and heaven; sang

Of things unknown that stand behind and 'fore

The lampless doors of death and birth; he sang

Of mystery, and wonderment, of time,

Firm law, fair liberty; of God, and fate;

Of love also, of love that never held

In his bright hands the dust of death, or pressed

His kisses on the lips of earthly maid;

Of love that leaneth to the shadowy arms

Of one whose face his blind eyes cannot see;

And fair immortal forms and fantasies,

Like insects rainbow-hued, and virgin-born,

With phantoms psyche-winged, took their life

And their aërial substance from the breath

Of his pure lips in singing; but no more

Was heard that plain and pastoral melody

Made of his voice and hers whom first he sang;

And some perceiving that his note was changed,

Reviled his heart's inconstancy, and swore

The very sweetness of the after-song

Was bitterness of falsehood; but none knew

The mystery of the song, or cared to hear

Its subtle delicacy of sound in sound,

Or see the beauty of the wingèd thought

Folded within its cradle chrysalis

Of language; of his mystic love alway

He sang, with his strange music wandering

The land; but kindly looks he met from none

Save from those kindred eyes to whom he made

Her image, in the setting of his song,

Apparent, in that beauty wherewithal

He held it in his soul, and steadfast bore

Through all the turmoil of that time, when men

Rose up against the poet — for he heard

Her voice above the clangour of the crowd —

"Follow the eastern star, and thou shalt find

My birthplace and my home, and what had been

Place of my death, had I not heard thy voice

Call to me in the sorrow of thy dream,

And came; though saving thee, none hath

  desired,

And none hath known me in thy land, towards

which

The sun of my land travelleth to set."

And then the sound would cease and come again,

Like the continuous sweetness of a dream

After the lapse of sleep, "Fear not, but hope;

As once in brighter hours thou didst desire

To seek the river-sources, and to see

Another country, wilt thou follow far,

Where'er my light shall lead? although not yet

Thou see'st my face, and though not at all times

I shall be with thee; for when in thine eyes

The light of day is strongest, and thine ears

Are filled with hearing, then my form shall fade

Out of thy sight, and thou shalt lose my voice

In sounds of earth. Fear not my vanishing;

For being gone, when I shall come again

I shall be dearer; lest the soul should faint

And weary of my presence, and mine eyes'

Continual on-looking, as of old

They wearied." So he faltered not, but strove;

New hope being his, and strength of victory

In joy consuming sorrow, and in life

O'ercoming powers of death; and a new song

Was on his lips of faithfulness and praise;

Though sometimes with its harmonies he wove

Majestic discords of his hate and scorn;

As thus, of faith — "True faith to falsehood

   bound

Is mere unfaithfulness; better to break

With falsehood, and be true: that one I loved —

Fair as the faint false sunset in the east

That takes the last light of the sunken sun

From clouds that shroud him dying, false as fair

Was she!"

      Thus singing toward the twilight hills

He travelled onward, still pursued, and spent

With combating the mad uncertain crowd.

But when the door was shut, and the lamp dim,

And the faint fire upon the hearth was low —

Life low — sense shut and dim; she would appear

As light in outer darkness, and his soul

Was filled with seeing; but when in his eyes

The light of day was strongest, and his ears

Were filled with hearing, then her form would fade

Out of his sight, and he would lose her voice

In sounds of earth, and unto her would cry:

"Flee, and I follow! and if dreadful day

Doth drive thee from me, then my soul shall go

To meet dark night upon the twilight hills,

Shadowing an awful bridal; or if thou

Desire me not, beloved, I am fain

Only to live, and stretch mine arms, and feel

After thy dark embrace, and can endure

To find them touch and close, and beat in vain

On mine own barren breast; I will not fear,

If sometime in my dreams I have the hope

Of thy beloved appearing; for my soul,

Untouched by weakness of these lips and eyes,

And hands that were another's, all in all

Is thine; and never in the former years

Loved, save in semblance." Thus, though sore
    beset

And harassed by the blasphemies that howled

Against him, and the legend of his love;

(For her whose face their undesiring eyes

Had never seen, their evil lips denied;

And, of her likeness in his soul, if one

Believed his saying, that one was swift to swear

It was a lying image, sent to lure

His heart from constancy) at last he reached

A city on the border of the hills;

And in the darkened streets at evening

He wandered; till within a silent square

He stood, where marble statues of great men

Were gathered — statesmen, warriors of old —

Waste was their place, and dim, and all around

Their eyes from lowering laurels looked at him,

And their cold fingers, with the dusty scrolls

They held, ne'er ceased to point their cruel scorn:

Here, to the music of his lips and lyre

There thronged a fearful crowd that filled the
  square;

And in clusters of wild faces hung and peered

From every window; and on every roof

The mad swarm clung — pale forms of hate and
  pain,

And phantom-handed fears, and Ignorance,

A fearful shape, came banded with the force

Of sightless Custom cowled; and, as he sang

They stretched their fingers towards his laurel
  crown,

And tore it from him; when he would have
  turned

To look on her of whom his eyes had hope

Dimly, as of a dream that breaks a dream,

To comfort its delirium — behold!

The blinded senses rose and smote his soul,

And turned it from her.

                    Then o'ercome he sank,

And, as all low in dust their victim lay,

The conquering crowd drew back, and left him
  lone,

Under the stolid statues where he fell,

With his rent wreath for pillow; and more late,

The sweet rare ministers of Love and Hope,

And gentle dreams stole visiting, to cast

Their light on the sad Hours that watched with
  him.

And at the last came Death, and lo! his brows

Were crowned with amaranth, and by the hand

He led that damsel of the poet's dream,

Towards whom his hope and passion ever

  yearned

To see her form unveiled; as she drew near

His weak hands grasped the border of her veil,

And as his eyes grew 'ware of that device

Encharactered thereon, he read the sign

And self-same symbol of his former fear —

"Thou knowest me not, I am not that I seem."

And Death, advancing, lifted up the veil —

Then his dim eyes beholding, scarce endured

The mingled splendour of the twain,

  transformed,

And seen as one — his first and latest love;

Of mystery unspeakable, yet bright

With an immortal brilliance, that consumed

The shade of Death beside her. As he gazed,

The dying poet's lips a little while

Stirred with their breath the hovering air, then

  spake,

"If any singer shall come after me,

Tell him, ye listening Hours that watch my

　death,

The twain I loved, if that himself shall love

In the hereafter, are but one; so seen

In diverse seeming — for as best the soul

Can bear to look on Nature, she appears;

And the desire of some is satisfied

With all of her the which their eyes can see,

And their hands handle, eager to embrace

Her beauty as a bride; while some there are

Who see all things in thought, and thought in

　all,

Who inly-looking have not failed to find

Her form within the light of their own dreams,

And worship her with reverence. I myself,

In my imperfect vision, did divide

That Being, and my spirit but desired

According to its knowledge; now I know

That One, the manifold in seeming fair!

For dear life's sake itself the soul doth cling

Unto the object of its sweet desire;

For they are wed together; if the one

Should flee, the other must pursue; if one

Should change, the other changeth; for indeed

The very law of life that binds in one

The outer and the inner, needeth this;

For, as the body lives by food, the soul,

In love and thought subsisting, when whate'er

Supplies that love shall fail, itself must cease;

So each by other lives, and love in them

Is the sweet interchange of life with life.

Tell him, that singer that shall follow me,

If thou wouldst live, love that which cannot die,

For when thou lovest not thy song shall cease;

Therefore 'tis vain to let the heart die down

In the dark grave of a dead love, if so

The more life thou dost gain in loving more,

Or — if he'd have it thus — in knowing more.

To seek, to find, to lose, and find again;

To break thy folly's faith to falsehood sworn;

To hope, to love, to hate, and love again,

Through all the dreary round of earthly days

Seemeth inconstant, yet is constancy

To that which is the being of all truth,

Beauty, and love, one soul in many forms!"

Dying, or rather living — following

Love led by happy Death — the poet ceased

From his last singing.

                        There is yet a song

Which they who know it call the "Song of

  Death,"

Sung by Apollodorus; or, some say

Made by a later singer of the land

Who loved the poet; as it is, it keeps

Sweet record of his dying music, borne

O'er land and sea by the sad Hours, bereft

Of borrowed splendour, loving him who sang

Bent down in patient hearkening; afterwards

Echoing the sounds it loved and treasured then,

E'en as the tender spiral of the shell

Treasures the dead voice of a silent sea.

MISCELLANEOUS POEMS.

GEORGE ELIOT.

Shalt thou not live, great soul, for evermore?

Whether, through some precipitate new birth,

Urged, in a distant heaven or vaster earth,

To living form and semblance as before;

Or whether — so to BE henceforth, and SEEM

No longer — like a dream, that worn and dim

With the awakening morning, on the verge

Of consciousness first dieth, thou didst merge

Thyself in the Self-consciousness of Him —

The Unknown, the Unimagined, the Unmade,

Himself the life and death, the light and shade,

The substance, and the shadow, and the dream;

Or whether we speak truth who speak of thee

As dead — dead star! thy light shall point their
   morn
To souls whose generations are unborn,
Travelling through years which seem eternity,
From thy death-region distant and forlorn.

What if the light that shone about thee here,
The circling splendour of thine earthly fame,
Showed to the world the wrong it had not seen,
But for that glory, if it brought more near
Thy presence to the vulgar eyes, thy name
To lips which censured faults that had not been,
But for thy perilous station, for the stress
Of thy life's need in that high loneliness?
Oh! soul so strong — yet woman-weak to lean
On man's firm heart! that 'mid its greatness
   found
No rest, till fainting life with love was crowned,
As with its flower.

      For not that thou wast sage

Alone, with that calm science used to gauge

The pulses of man's passion, being full

Of large experience, and apt to show

The love, the sorrow, the mistake, the toil

Of simple lives that grow on English soil;

With art that takes the commonplace, the dull,

The homely form and speech, the trivial thing

Of everyday, making it beautiful;

Not for this only — but that thou didst know

The heart's still tragedy of strife and pain,

And woman's hopeless wrong and suffering,

Vague yearnings and lame motions after good,

Ardour, devotion — ay, for this we deem

Thee great; as not alone in power and brain

And utterance of knowledge thou didst seem

Manlike, but wiser in thy womanhood.

Shalt thou not live hereafter? In the sphere

Made brighter by the light thou hast not hid,

In thoughts made vaster for thy thinking, deeds

Made nobler by the deeds thy heroes did,

In lives made higher by thy aims, in creeds

Made wiser for thy tolerance — whene'er

Some love-crost girl hath raised her golden head

From love-tale of thy telling, comforted;

Where suffering hearts have been and yet shall

   be,

Whom thou hast taught with power and

   tenderness;

Revealing in fair words and images

Love — Duty — Truth — a threefold sanctity.

A FABLE.

Fair Truth lay at the bottom of a well

   Where all who came to draw the water, leant

To find her where she lurked, invisible,

   Deep down — but on the surface, as he bent,

Brooding on that clear darkness, each descried

   The image of *himself* reflected there,

And at the sight went forth, full satisfied,

Crying, "I have seen the Truth, and she is fair!

THE SINGER.

"WHAT is the message thou bearest, brought
From over the land, from under the sea?
What is the song and the secret, taught,
   Singer, to thee?"

"Mine is the message of love to the bride,
My song is sweet with her secret said, —
Bitter with breath of her lips that sighed
   When love lay dead.

"Mine is the message of heaven to earth,
Heard from the hill-tops, heard from afar,
Told in the time when the day hath birth

At the death of the star.

"My song is caught from the song of a bird,

Singing in summer, sweet singing to me;

My secret is that which the shore hath heard

From the mouth of the sea.

"I bear the message of hope and faith,

Of all that from doubt and despair is born,

As love from sorrow, as life from death,

From the night — the morn!"

IMMORTELLE.

With uncouth grass and weeds
  Is all my garden grown —
Thistles whose feathered seeds
  By random winds were sown;

All bitter herbs, and dark
  Nightshades of poison breath;
With nettles venomous; and stark,
  Black cypresses for death.

But in a quiet spot
  Groweth and blossometh well
One flower-like star that setteth not,

Which men call "Immortelle."

That garden knows no sun,

But love, life, light thou art,

Bright blossom and star in one! —

That garden is my heart.

EUTHANASIA.

WHAT wouldst thou carry over unto death,

If death know aught of aught that life held dear?

Soul! what wouldst thou take with thee? Not

   the breath

Of sweetest earthly songs, when thou mayest

   hear

Songs beyond death, sweeter than life e'er sung;

Oh! nought of faiths or facts sore wretched and

   wrung

From dark experience, mixed and manifold,

Knowing the truth wherein all truths are one;

Nor fruit, nor crown of labour and deeds done

In life, in death's life wouldst thou keep and

hold.

But — for thou goest hence friendless and
alone —

Of all thou knewest bear to the Unknown

These — the last smile a mother gave to thee;

The impress of the touch of human hands;

Remembered voices of the wind and sea;

The look of sunset over happy lands;

And sweet, last kiss of love that ceased to be.

CHRISTAPOLLO.

In Memoriam Percy Bysshe Shelley.

A singer in a dream did stand,

  Between the darkness and the day,

The morning star at his left hand;

Upon the limit of the land,

  A fair, yet fearful form; one way

He looked, he held a lyre, and tried

  Its golden pulses, ere he sang;

And, while his voiceless prelude died

In fainting echoes, rarified

  To silence, through the twilight rang

A Voice, that stayed the breath that hung

On his wild lips in rapture, ere

It passed into divinest song;

Saying, "Let no music from thy tongue

    Be born, until thy spirit shall swear —

"Steadfast to stand, and ill-bestead,

    To battle against envious powers;

To fail not, hissed and buffeted,

Pursued, and stung in heart or head

    By arrows of the blinding hours;

"To adorn with love thy misery,

    Even as a bride, until delight

Is born of her; or bound, to be

In thy captivity yet free;

    Defenceless, pledge thyself to fight

"Against all sceptred ignorance,

    All mitred falsehood, crownèd hate

Whate'er; to defy change and chance,

And custom, and vile circumstance —

   Tyrannicide of thy own fate.

"To know and reverence above

   All else the greatest, nor forget

The least; to let thy spirit move

Betwixt the embrace of hope and love,

   Beloved of both; or, harder yet,

"To love, where Love hath ceased to live;

   To hope, where Hope becomes Despair;

Aye unforgiven, to forgive;

To look on evil, yet believe

   No less in divine things and fair;

"To wake, though the world's night be long,

   An eye in darkness, and a voice

In silence; wandering with thy song

The languid, twilight dreams among
    Of sleeping spirits, till they rejoice.

"This is to find what thou hast sought —
    The poet's empire; this, to be
The lord or god of thine own thought!"
He swore, his keen voice faltered not;
    Then in that dream's immensity

He faded — from his lips and lyre
    Burst music, as he passed away
Crowned; into spikèd flames like briar
His splendour split, and faint with fire
    Of dawn, died in the burning day.